Space, in Chains

Books by Laura Kasischke

LAURA KASISCHKE

Space, in Chains

Copper
Canyon
Press

Port Townsend, Washington

Printed in the United States of America

Cover art: Mark Rothko, *Number 8,* 1952. © 2010 Kate Rothko Prizel & Christopher Rothko / Artists Rights Society (ARS), New York

Copper Canyon Press is in residence at Fort Worden State Park in Port Townsend, Washington, under the auspices of Centrum. Centrum is a gathering place for artists and creative thinkers from around the world, students of all ages and backgrounds, and audiences seeking extraordinary cultural enrichment.

LIBRARY OF CONGRESS CATALOGING-IN-PUBLICATION DATA

Kasischke, Laura, 1961–
Space, in chains / Laura Kasischke.
   p.   cm.
ISBN 978-1-55659-333-8 (pbk.: alk. paper)
I. Title.
PS3561.A6993S63 2011
811´.54–dc22

2010040037

9 8 7 6 5 4 3 2 FIRST PRINTING

Copper Canyon Press
Post Office Box 271
Port Townsend, Washington 98368

www.coppercanyonpress.org

for Lucy & Jack

Flying swiftly past,
For a child I last forever,
For adults I'm gone too fast...

ACKNOWLEDGMENTS

I am grateful to the Guggenheim Foundation for a fellowship that supported the completion of this book, as well as United States Artists for a generous USA Cummings Fellowship.

Thank you to the editors of the following publications, in which these poems originally appeared:

The Adirondack Review: "Stolen shoes"

Boston Review: "Mercy"

Chautauqua: "My son makes a gesture my mother used to make"

Conduit: "Cytoplasm, June"

Dunes Review: "Dawn," "Lunch," "O elegant giant (These difficult matters)"

Field: "Landscape with one of the earthworm's ten hearts"

Gulf Coast: "The key to the tower," "Your headache"

Harvard Review: "Abigor"

Hayden's Ferry Review: "Space, in chains"

The Iowa Review: "The call of the one duck flying south," "Song"

The Kenyon Review: "At the public pool," "My beautiful soul"

The Laurel Review: "Animal, vegetable, mineral, mist"

Luna: "You"

The Missouri Review: "My father's mansion"

Narrative: "Atoms on loan," "Life support," "The photograph album in the junk shop," "Tools and songs"

New American Writing: "O elegant giant (And Jehovah)" (Reprinted in *The Pushcart Prize XXXIV*)

New England Review: "Almost there," "Rain," "Riddle (I am the mirror)," "Riddle (Most days)," "They say"

New Letters: "Four Men" "Riddle (Mars, the moon)"

Poetry: "After Ken Burns," "Hospital parking lot, April," "Look"

POOL: "Recipe for disaster"

Puerto del Sol: "The Pleasure Center"

Redivider: "Forgiveness"

Salamander: "Pharmacy," "Receipt"

Smartish Pace: "Dread"

The Southern Review: "Memory of grief," "My son practicing the violin," "Swan logic," "We watch my father try to put on his shirt"

TriQuarterly: "Riddle (The bodies of the girls)," "The sweet by-and-by"

Willow Springs: "Near misses"

When I came in my son said, "Mother, something has come down from Mars and the world is coming to an end." I said, "Don't be silly." Then my husband said, "It is true."

> Bury deep
> Pile on stones,
> Yet I will
> Dig up the bones.
> What am I?

CONTENTS

One

Two

Three

Space, in Chains

ONE

O elegant giant

And Jehovah. And Alzheimer. And a diamond of extraordinary size on the hand of a starving child. The quiet mob in a vacant lot. My father asleep in a chair in a warm corridor. While his boat, the Unsinkable, sits at the bottom of the ocean. While his boat, the Unsinkable, waits marooned on the shore. While his boat, the Unsinkable, sails on, and sails on.

Riddle

I am the mirror breathing above the sink.
There is a censored garden inside of me.
Over my worms someone has thrown

a delicately embroidered sheet.

And also the child at the rummage sale—

more souvenirs than memories.

I am the cat buried beneath
the tangled ivy. Also the white
weightless egg
floating over its grave. Snow

where there were leaves. Empty
plastic cups after the party on the beach.

I am ash rising above a fire, like a flame.
The Sphinx with so much sand
blowing vaguely in her face. The last

shadow that passed
over the blank canvas
in the empty art museum. I am

the impossibility of desiring
the person you pity.
And the petal of the Easter lily—

That ghost of a tongue.
That tongue of a ghost.

What would I say if I spoke?

Memory of grief

I remember a four-legged animal strolling through a fire. Poverty in a prom dress. A girl in a bed trying to tune the AM radio to the voices of the dead. A temple constructed out of cobwebs into which the responsibilities of my daily life were swept. Driving through a Stop sign waving to the woman on the corner, who looked on, horrified.

But I remember, too, the way,
loving everyone equally because each of us would die,
I walked among the crowds of them, wearing
my disguise.
And how, when it was over, I found myself
here again
with a small plastic basket on my arm, just

another impatient immortal
sighing and fidgeting in an unmoving line.

Song

The floor of the brain, the roof
of the mouth, the locked
front door, the barn
burned down, a dog
tied to a tree, not howling, a dark
shed, an empty garage, a basement
in which a man might sip
his peace, in peace,
and a table
in a kitchen
at which
the nightingales feasted on fairy tales,
the angels stuffed themselves with fog

And a tiny room at the center of it all,
and a beautiful woman the size of a matchstick
singing the song that ruined my father:

his liver
his life

The kind of song a quiet man
might build a silent house around

Time

Like a twentieth-century dream of Europe—all
horrors, and pastries—some part of me, for all time
stands in a short skirt in a hospital cafeteria line, with a tray, while

in another glittering tower named
for the world's richest man
my mother, who is dying, never dies.

(Bird
with one wing
in Purgatory, flying in circles.)

I wake up decades later, having dreamt I was crying.
My alarm clock seconds away
from its own alarm.

I wake up to its silence
every morning
at the same hour. The daughter
of the owner of the Laundromat
has washed my sheets in tears

and the soldiers marching across some flowery field in France
bear their own soft pottery in their arms—heart, lung, abdomen.

And the orderlies and the nurses and their clattering
carts roll on and on. In a tower. In a cloud. In a cafeteria line.

See, cold spy for time, who needs you now?

After Ken Burns

The beautiful plate I cracked in half as I wrapped it in tissue paper—

as if the worship of a thing might be the thing that breaks it.

This river, which is life, which is wayfaring. This river,
which is also sky. This dipper, full of mind, which is

not only the hysterical giggling of girls, but the trembling
of the elderly. Not only
the scales, beaks, and teeth of creatures but also
their imaginative names (*elephant, peacock*) and their
love of one another, the excited
preparations they sometimes make for their own deaths.

It is as if some graceful goddess, wandering in the dark, desperate with thirst,
bent down and dropped that dipper
clumsily in this river. It floated away. *Consciousness, memory, sensory
        information, the*
historians
and their glorious war...

The pineal gland, tiny pinecone in the forehead, our third eye:

Of course, it will happen here. No doubt. Someday, here,
in this little house, they will lay the wounded
side by side. The blood
will run into the basement through the boards. Their

ghosts are already here, along
with the cracked plate wrapped in old paper
in the attic,

and the woman who will turn one day at the window to see
a long strange line of vehicles traveling slowly toward her door, which

she opens (what choice does she have?) although
she has not yet been born.

My beautiful soul

It is the beggar who thanks me profusely for the dollar.
It is a boat of such beggars sinking
beneath the weight of this one's thanking.

It is the bath growing cold around the crippled woman
calling to someone in another room.

And the arthritic children in the park
picking dust off summer
speck by speck
while a bored nurse watches.

The wind has toppled the telescope
over onto the lawn:
So much for stars.
Your brief shot at the universe, gone.

It is some water lilies and a skull in a decorative pond,
and a tiny goldfish swimming
like an animated change-purse
made of brightness and surprises
observing the moment through its empty eye.

Thank you, thank you, bless you, beautiful
lady with your beautiful soul...
It is as if I have tossed a postcard
of the ocean into the ocean.

My stupid dollar, my beautiful soul.

The photograph album in the junk shop

We are all the same, it claims. This
forgotten couple kissing
before the Christmas tree, in a year
they will be holding
the Christ child between them, whose
name they wish us to believe
is *Jim.*

Someone with a wheel.
A girl in a purple dress, squinting.
A wolf
rolling in ashes. A cake
bearing the Christ child's name. The waterfall
at the center of every life
spewing foam and beauty
onto the boats below. And also
the canyon into which will slip—

What is this on the rocks below?

The whole damn picnic?

And the shadow of that terrible
animal with horns
at every petting zoo. And
the Christ child in a costume
smoking cigarettes. The poisonous
brambles in bloom on a chain-link fence. A fat
man pretends to fly. A blond

woman laughs at a hand. The scoreboard. The lawn
mown. The family cat. (Here,
it is Acceptance. Here,
Malice.)
And beside them all, there is
Grandma

in a chair
staring at the future as she tells
a story without moving her lips. It is

a story to which the family
doesn't listen
because they are too busy
doing what families do.

And because it can't be true.

And still
her face waits on every page
like an ax left behind on the moon.

Landscape with one of the earthworm's ten hearts

and also a small boy with a golden crossbow,
and a white rabbit full of arrows.
Also snow. And the sky, of course, the color
of a gently stirred winter soup.

I am the inert figure behind the barren apple tree.
The one who wonders for what purpose
the real world was created. I ruin everything by being in it, while one
of the earthworm's hearts, deep in the ground, fills up the rest
of the landscape with longing, and fiery collisions, and caves
full of credit cards and catalogues. You can tell

I hear it, too, by the look on my face:

That inaudible thumping insisting without believing
one is enough is enough is enough.

The inner workings

This afternoon my son tore
his shorts climbing a barbed-wire fence. *Holy Toledo,* I said
when he crashed back through the cornstalks
with half of his shorts gone.

The sun was ringing its sonorous silent bell underground, as someone's
grandmother tucked
an awful little cactus under
a doily embroidered with buttercups.

In prisons

exhausted prisoners napped, having
brief and peaceful dreams, while beautiful girls in bikinis tossed
fitfully in their own shadows
on a beach

and somewhere else
in some man's secret garden shed
the watchmaker, the lens maker, the radio-

maker, the maker
of telescopes, of rhetorical devices:

The time-maker, the eye-maker, the voice-maker, the maker
of stars, of space, of comic surprises

bent together
over the future

clumsily tinkering with the inner
workings of its delights.

Hospital parking lot, April

Once there was a woman who laughed for years uncontrollably
after a stroke.

Once there was a child who woke after surgery to find his parents
were impostors.

These seagulls above the parking lot today, made of hurricane and
ether, they

have flown directly out of the brain wearing little blue-gray masks,
like strangers' faces, full

of wingèd mania, like television in waiting rooms. Entertainment.
Pain. The rage

of fruit trees in April, and your car, which I parked in a shadow
before you died, decorated now with feathers,
and unrecognizable

with the windows unrolled
and the headlights on
and the engine still running
in the Parking Space of the Sun.

View from glass door

I have stood here before.
Just this morning
I reached into the dark of the dishwasher
and stabbed my hand with a kitchen knife.

Bright splash of blood on the kitchen
floor. Astonishing
red. (All
that brightness inside me?)

My son, the Boy Scout, ran
to get the First Aid kit—while, beyond
the glass door, the orchard. Beyond

the orchard, the garden bed, and

beyond the garden, all
the simple people I remember
simply standing in their lines.
Or sitting in their chairs
waiting for the film to start
or for the plane to land
or for the physician to call them in.

How easy it would have been instead
to stand up shouting
about cold, dumb death.

But there they waited
as if the credits
might begin to roll again.
As if the bandages, the bolts, the scrolls. The paper
towels, the toilet paper. And

as the family stood around
considering my hand, I could clearly hear

the great silenced choirs of them
singing soothing songs:

Who fended for
and fed me. Who
lay beside me in the dark and
stroked my head. Who

called me their sweetheart, their
miracle child. Who
taught me to love
by loving me. Who, by dying, taught
me to die.

Covered in earth.
Covered in earth.
On the other side
of this glass door.
Calm, memorized
faces to the sky.

July

July, that lovely hell, all
velvet dresses and drapes
stuffed into a hot little hole.

July trampled by the sweat and froth
of panicked circus animals.
You think, *Romantic*
overload. She
exaggerates. Melodrama, menopause, but no:

I was there, where the pale words, like light on a wave.
Where the forgotten ancient music was still played.

The lovers, gone. Their beds unmade. Their
pets in cages. Where the primal. Where the blur.
Where the tamed

bear, the injured bird of prey, maddened nocturnal animals
roaming the streets in the heat of the day.

And that girl there:

The chaplain's little book of her, slammed
shut, as she
sits on the front stoop
painting her nails.
Sipping lemonade.
Just that age

when the cool, empty vestibules
are still behind you
in which one day
such desperate bargains
and trades will be made.

Wasps

I stumbled into this place with my suitcase packed full of prior obligations. The floor of the orchard littered with soft fruit, and the wasps hovering drunkenly over it all, and the last few pieces dangling from the branches —happiness, melancholy, sexual desire—poised in the vibrating air, ready to fall.

These systems already existed. So what did they want from me? The deep, deep cosmogony. The rigorous mimicry of genes. Algebra, democracy, infectious diseases. Farm implements, logic, religious convictions. A stick in the river. Music. Linguistics. *Sweetheart, it's time to leave...*

But, first:

A bus ride to the beach! My mother in a striped suit, with black hair. June. A pail full of sand and water. In the distance, someone on a boat, waving. The crippled girl floating on her back. The old man and the silvery blue consummation, laughing happily, up to his ankles, smiling at me. And my dead grandmother and her simple picnic. Some fruit. Cheese. Some cold fried chicken. The physical universe and its buzzing machinery, its fantastical scenery.

They were all around us that day. In the confusion of air. In our strange dreams. In the baggage we'd brought with us and would have to leave. In our fading animal memories:

The humming gold of being, and ceasing to be. The exposed motor of eternity.

Dawn

She was my friend who went crazy.
She was my crazy friend. Was

she crazy that day on the way to the lake, at

the mall, the luncheonette, my
bridal shower—was she crazy then?

Nights, the stolen babies sleep
so peacefully in the arms of their thieves.
Please, mothers, don't scream when we take them.
Please, mothers, don't scream you will wake them.

While, outside in the dark is the guest
whose invitation we forgot to send.
In the morning we'll find him
asleep in our bed. Consequence

itself. Itself, and Regret.

Look

Look! I bear into this room a platter piled high with the rage my mother felt toward my father! Yes, it's diamonds now. It's pearls, public humiliation, an angry dime-store clerk, a man passed out at the train station, a girl at the bookstore determined to read every fucking magazine on this shelf for free. They tell us that most of the billions of worlds beyond ours are simply desolate oceanless forfeits in space. But logic tells us there *must* be operas, there *have* to be car accidents cloaked in that fog. Down here, God just spit on a rock, and it became a geologist. God punched a hole in the drywall on Earth and pulled out of that darkness another god. She—

just kept her thoughts to herself. She just—

followed him around the house, and every time he turned a light on, she turned it off.

Rain

The sun, made of water, like all
the secrets made of tongues—
it falls all night, and in the morning
the flames have been put out

and the stones, bewitched, can see:

The lost hours, and into the past.
The memories of infants, of cats, of
other stones—that they have souls.
That they *are* souls.

And the terror of foxes.
And the children's hospital.
And the hangman's alarm clock.
And the official on the doorstep.

And all the embezzled
cents and dollars
of the last time I saw you.

Peace

The boy climbs the tree that will be his ruin, and the ruin of his generation. The view from the top too dazzling to see. The air too bright to breathe. And the box inside him in which his mother resides is velvet and black and without size. And the nation waits in a shadow. And a baby about to be born is weighted down instead with a stone:

The tree, the boy, the celebrity divorce. The palace with all that blood spilled all over that marble floor: At the library again today, as at the car dealership and the grocery store, no one says a word about the war.

Pharmacy

A knife plunged into the center
of summer. Air

and terror, which become teeth together.

The pearl around which the sea
formed itself into softly undulating song—

This tender moment when my father
gives a package of cookies to my son.

They have been saved
from the lunch tray
for days.

Hook
in a sponge. The expressions on both of their faces. A memory I will carry
with me always, and which will sustain me, despite all the years I will try to
prescribe this memory away.

Medical dream

I open the door on a Sunday morning
to roses. The door
of my little cottage, my little door, choked
with roses. This

start of a tale about bewilderment, fatigue. The trees

in their temporary trances, and we in our animate brevity:

Health, there is no army for it. No
bus pass. No
factory.

It is the key
made of shadow
to the car that won't start.
The slow rolling of the cement truck through town.

It is God
lasering His way across a landscape
littered with other gods. Their huge, lunatic dreams.

My clothes on a hook.
My body on a table. A knock
on my front door, and

Lazarus, the florist, delivering
roses

from relatives
from friends:

Lazarus, who surely never dared
to lay his head
on a pillow
and close his eyes again.

Near misses

The truck that swerved to miss the stroller in which I slept.

My mother turning from the laundry basket just in time to see me open the third-story window to call to the cat.

In the car, on ice, something spinning and made of history snatched me back from the guardrail and set me down between two gentle trees. And that time I thought to look both ways on the one-way street.

And when the doorbell rang, and I didn't answer, and just before I slipped one night into a drunken dream, I remembered to blow out the candle burning on the table beside me.

It's a miracle, I tell you, this middle-aged woman scanning the cans on the grocery store shelf. Hidden in the works of a mysterious clock are her many deaths, and yet the whole world is piled up before her on a banquet table again today. The timer, broken. The sunset smeared across the horizon in the girlish cursive of the ocean, *Forever, For You.*

And still she can offer only her body as proof:

The way it moves a little slower every day. And the cells, ticking away. A crow pecking at a sweater. The last hour waiting patiently on a tray for her somewhere in the future. The spoon slipping quietly into the beautiful soup.

The key to the tower

There was never
There was never
A key to the tower

There was never a key to the tower, you fool

It was a dream
It was a dream
A mosquito's dream

A mosquito dreaming in a cage for a bird

It's October
It's October
The summer's over

Your passionate candle in a pumpkin's head
And the old woman's hand in this photograph
Appears to be nailed to the old man's hand

And the sky
And the sky
And the sky above you

Is a drunken loved one asleep in your bed

And the tower
And the tower
And the key to the tower

There was never a key to the tower I said

And this insistence
This insistence
It will only bring you sorrow

Your ridiculous key, your laughable tower

But there was
There was
A tower here

I swear

And the key
And the key
I still have it here somewhere

Space, in chains

Things that are beautiful, and die. Things that fall asleep in the afternoon, in sun. Things that laugh, then cover their mouths, ashamed of their teeth. A strong man pouring coffee into a cup. His hands shake, it spills. His wife falls to her knees when the telephone rings. *Hello? Goddammit, hello?*

Where is their child?

Hamster, tulips, love, gigantic squid. *To live.* I'm not endorsing it.

Any single, transcriptional event. The chromosomes of the roses. Flagella, cilia, all the filaments of touching, of feeling, of running your little hand hopelessly along the bricks.

Sky, stamped into flesh, bending over the sink to drink the *tour de force* of water.

It's all space, in chains—the chaos of birdsong after a rainstorm, the steam rising off the asphalt, a small boy in boots opening the back door, stepping out, and someone calling to him from the kitchen,

Sweetie, don't be gone too long.

We watch my father try to put on his shirt

Somewhere, my dead mother kneels at a trunk, her head and her arms all the way up as she tosses things over her shoulders, and cries.

The letters, the fading. The labyrinth, the cake. The four hundred brackish lakes of the brain. She searches for the
music, but she can't find it. Oh, God, it was here
only the other day.

He cannot do it. The shirt
slips to the floor. There is
dancing and laughter in hell, an angel weeping openly on a park bench in heaven. My mother, dead and frantic in an attic. A white shirt on a floor. An old man in a wheelchair, rubbing his eyes. *Here it is, here it is!* the occupational therapists sing as they rise to the surface of the earth, smiling, bearing their terrible surprise.

The call of the one duck flying south

so far behind the others
in their neat little *v*, in their
competence of plans and wings, if
you didn't listen you would think
it was a cry for help
or sympathy—
friends! friends!—
but it isn't.

Silence of the turtle on its back in the street.
Silence of the polar bear pulling its wounded weight onto the ice.
Silence of the antelope with a broken leg.
Silence of the old dog asking for no further explanation.

How
was it I believed I was
God's favorite creature? I,
who carry my feathery skeleton across the sky now, calling
out for all of us. I, who am doubt now, with a song.

TWO

Your headache

I am trying to imagine it
Your head is in your hands
The nurse is pouring pills onto a plate
November again
Too late

Your headache
It is a bird
Wounded, in leaves

Its sweet bird's nest is full of pain in a distant place

November
There are daisies
In the ruined garden, still blooming strangely

And in a manic yellow hat, the old lady

And the old man, dead in his bed

And their daughter, the saint:

Her dark, religious hair gets tangled in the branches
She is screaming, grabbing

While the nurses play Mozart in another room
While the bats fly over the roof
Snatch the black notes from the blackness
Laughing

You cry
I am going to die

I can see them through this window

Their little black capes

The touching ugliness of their little faces

Space, between humans & gods

The day
en route to darkness. The guillotine
on the way to the neck. The train
to nudity. The bus
to being alone. The main-and-mast,
and the thousand oars, the
thousand hands.

And the ship sailing on
toward the glory and the gone.

And you, too, my beautiful one, having
outgrown another
pair of shoes,
tossing them into the box
we've named Goodwill.

And then the donkey ride to Bethlehem.
The long slow process of boarding the plane.
And my father

ringing the bell for the nurse
in the night, and then

not even the bell. Ringing

the quiet. Waiting
in the silence

as she travels toward him across it

wearing her white.

Swan logic

Swan terror and swan stigmata. Three of them slaughtered
at the edge of the pond
and one still

One still gliding in wounded circles on the black mirror of that, like
some music box tragedy inside some girl.

Or the swan inside the dying man pacing the hallways with a ball and chain.

Feathers in the road. One still

One still trying to drag itself back
to that black glass.

Incoming, the nurse says
referring to the minivan. *We*

must prepare the tables. We shall wear white.

The mother

The mother was drunk.

The children were killed.

Except for one

Except for one.

At the fair, the wild lights.

Lace your shoes up little darlings.
I'll take you there tonight

There, tonight. The eternity of that. Swan logic. Swan history. The white

tents on fire. The air-raid sirens. The bloodied
brides. The grand hotels. The outgoing tides. The slow
progress of certain diseases. The urgent warnings

The urgent warnings:

The dreamy terror of certain summer mornings.
Swan God, who

God, who—

Who shot our swans. Who
was a decent man. Who
loved his family. Who
could not bear to watch them suffer. Who
killed them lovingly one by one.

Swan boats.

Swan souls. Swans

in cages, in trunks, in boxes, in plastic bags. Swans still dragging. Swans
still circling. Swan
still

Swan stillness and swan slaughter still circling the center of the swan.

Riddle

Mars, the moon, the man hammering on the roof all afternoon. The Greenwich clock, the worker bees, the agitated bubbles in a stream. They have a plan, these:

Theirs is the world of the railing nailed down around the canyon for the sightseeing blind.

A woman sprawls out on a beach with a book, ready to read, but, opening it, she sighs. *Oh my.* She has settled down on her towel with the life story of a fruit fly—

Believable, chronological, but so quickly erased that it only serves to prove that the universe is made of curving, warping space. That, if you think about order, it becomes disorder. That to want to succeed is to fail: The way those satellites pointed at the stars pick up no sound at all, except, every few decades, the discordant music of a few chickens in a cave.

Oh, yes, oh, yes, I see.

There is a bridge from here to there. But we all know it is the kind of bridge that blows away. The kind of bridge made mostly of magazines, cheap beer, TV.

Not built to weather much at all.
Not war, nor despair, nor disease.

Not even health. Not even peace.

There is a chasm beneath it, and on one side my father is in his hospital gown watching that bridge blow around in the breeze—and, on the other side, waiting, is the mysterious unknowable thing that might have made him happy in this life:

What if it was me?

The drinking couple, similes

Like the dead photographer's final image
of shadow and gravel, and then

that first drink, and suddenly we
were relaxing
like anchors
eyeless in the silence
of something like a sea

while we

were also clattering
crazily
over cobblestones, like carts
tied to runaway horses
in a fiery scene
from some old movie, and we

were also the directors
burning down the set

and also the horses
and the scenery

until the next drink

like a princess waking up
beside a chimpanzee—

or that chimpanzee
in a tuxedo, strapped

to a rocket, launched
in a living room, like

not the strong man's arm, just
the sleeve, as if

not only the birds but the cages
had been set free, the way we

were enjoying one another
enjoying one another's

company

like a couple separated by mirrors
straight down the center of a beach *(if*

you're having another one honey will
you pour another one for me?)

like a crate of crutches
washed up on that beach
or a kite brushing
a satellite, a star, a whole

solar system, while also
snagged by its tail in a tree

still drinking

like a couple of cars without drivers
dodging each other in the street

or laughing, shouting automatons

or butterflies landing
in wet cement, thinking
now we'll die

like party favors, as if we

were actual human beings
or completely normal people

until the last drink
when we

had no more need of similes.

Your last day

So we found ourselves in an ancient place, the very
air around us bound by chains. There was
stagnant water in which lightning
was reflected, like desperation
in a dying eye. Like science. Like
a dull rock plummeting through space, tossing
off flowers and veils, like a bride. And

also the subway.
Speed under ground.
And the way each body in the room appeared to be
a jar of wasps and flies that day—but, enchanted,
like frightened children's laughter.

O elegant giant

These difficult matters of grace and scale:

The way music, our savior, is the marriage of math and antisocial behavior.

Like this woman with a bucket in the morning gathering gorgeous oxymora on the shore...

And my wildly troubled love for you, which labored gently in the garden all through June, then tore the flowers up with its fists in July.

Which set a place for you next to mine—the fork beside the spoon beside the knife (the linen napkin, and the centerpiece: a blue beheaded blossom floating in a bowl)—and even the red weight of my best efforts poured into your glass as a dark wine before I tossed the table onto its side.

Just another perfect night. Beyond destruction, and utterly unlikely, how someone might have managed, blindly, to stumble on such a love in the middle of her life.

O elegant giant.

While, outside, the woods are silent.

And, overhead, not a single intelligent star in the sky.

At the public pool

I could carry my father in my arms.
I was a small child.
He was a large, strong man.
Muscled, tan.
But he felt like a bearable memory in my arms.

The lion covers his tracks with his tail.
He goes to the terrible Euphrates and drinks.
He is snared there by a little shrub.
The hunter hears his cries, and hurries for his gun.

What of these public waters?

Come in, I said to my little son.
He stood at the edge, looking down.
It was a slowly rolling mirror.
A strange blue porcelain sheet.
A naked lake, transparent as a need.

The public life.
The Radio Songs.
Political Art.
The Hall of Stuff We Bought at the Mall. The plugged-up fountain at
      the center
of the Museum of Crap That Couldn't Last
has flooded it all.

Come in, I said again. *In here you can carry your mother in your arms.*

I still see his beautiful belly forever.
The blond curls on his perfect head.
The whole Botticelli of it crawling on the surface
of the water. And
his sad, considerate expression.
No, he said.

My son makes a gesture my mother used to make

My son makes a gesture my mother used to make. The sun in their eyes. Fluttering their fingers. As if to disperse it. The sun, like so many feverish bees.

I keep driving. One eye on the road, and one on the child in the rearview mirror. A man on the radio praying. The awful kid down the block where I was a child who buried a toad in a jar in the sandbox, dug it up a month later, and it was still alive.

He does it again. The sun, like the drifting ashes of a distant past. The petals of some exploded yellow roses.

The miracle of it.
The double helix of it.
The water running uphill of it.
Such pharmacy, in a world which failed her! She died before he was even alive, and here she is again, shining in his eyes.

Light nodding to light.
Time waving hello to time.
The ninety-nine names of Allah.
The sun extravagantly bright and full of radiant, preposterous spiritual advice—like a Bible rescued from a fire that killed a family of five:

I squint into it and see both a glorious parade of extinct and mythological beasts, and an illustration in a textbook of a protective sheath of protein wrapped around a strand of DNA—all cartoon spirals and billiard balls, and the sole hope of our biology teacher, Mr. Barcheski, who, finally enraged by the blank expressions on our faces, slammed it shut and walked away.

Recipe for disaster

Too sweet, the ingredients. Too high the heat. From this ladder leaning against a cloud, I see the future—that luminous egg of the mouse and her lover the Wild White Bird.

Look what has hatched between them!

Deep time passes. Affection. Family. Herd animals and garden plants. And that woman balancing an exaggeration made of glass on her head. She's muttering something she overheard a girl once say to a steering wheel:

If you were so in love, why did you leave?

But she doesn't want to hear the answer to that question when the guy beside her opens his mouth to speak. Trust me.

Still, she grows older, and continues to believe. The gentle runners disappear behind the sun. War rolls down the side of the Mountain of Grief so peacefully.

And, swarming north today in the soft green of spring, those glittering killer bees. A mother now, she opens the door and sends her son scampering into the lovely hum with an empty jar and a kiss on the cheek.

Atoms on loan

for Bill

The eyelid of a stone in my hand

flutters, and then it opens. I say, *Hello?*

For a moment, I was a woman with her son standing under an arch made of ancient rocks in Scotland. (You took the photo.)

For an hour in 1981 I was a girl with drunken hair in a swaying tower.

For a month or two in my twenties I paddled a boat made of lead down a river of blood with my hands.

Once, I stood on a mountaintop gulping air from a cup *made* of that thin stuff. I drank so much I even drank the cup.

And, all that time, my bare feet in love with the ground. My green grapes scaling my green wall. My kite tangled in the highest wires, and something electrified into fire inside me.

And you, my shining Viking. You, my Viking's shining shield. You arguing with some other wife in some previous existence. The ivy splitting straight through the bricks. The children screaming obscenities on the beach. My father dragging on this lit cigarette for a century. Our son when he slips into the shadows of his classroom:

Maybe we can still hear his laughter, but we can't see him.

Who *are* we? Without one another,
who *were* we? Without one another,

who *will we be?*

Water washing away the flowers.
Flowers being taught how to speak.

You'll always remember me, my mother said, *but someday you'll no longer be sad about me.*

How could she have been so wrong?

How did she know?

Dread

How simple, the beheading. Dread

It is also an illusion—diseased internal organ
    floating in internal fog—You
    could stuff it back in after pulling it out
    or you could look at it carefully in the sun

It is also a projection—
    awful shadow puppet on an awful wall

Also, a god, all-powerful, with a voice, without a tongue

It is a season, too

The season in which you carry the dead thing
    up the mountain in your arms
    only to be given something squirming in a sack
    to carry back

Or the season in which you are given
    the incalculable sums
    and a lined piece of paper
    and nothing to write with. *Add it up*

Animal shudder. Something's coming

Wormwood

for C. Dale Young

That a star in heaven
might have poisonous feathers.
That an angel might cast it for
us into the sea.

So it is at the end of the oncology ward:
The little dish of complexion soap
beside the dying woman's bowl.

So it is at Chernobyl:
The Ferris wheel rusting
for decades in a forest.

The tiny shoes, the ruined reactor, the broken toys, the gas
masks hanging
from hooks on the back of the classroom door.

And the strong husband, the virtuous wife, the obedient
son and daughter, the brilliant
physician, the shadow
on the mammogram, the vault
full of wristwatches, lost, with one
still keeping perfect time

then stopping
at the moment—.

Also, the termite
gnawing at the foundation.

And the silent herds of reindeer
moving as
catastrophe through
the cool spring grasses of Scandinavia.

That it might have been foolish to fall in love with this world.
That God sent Word.
That the radiant dust of that
catastrophe
traveled for thousands
of miles on their fur.

That if God
were a man
who might have taken a lover, the lover

might have been you, iris, you

with a bright black beetle this morning
chewing religiously away at your beauty.

The sweet by-and-by

There is a place at the center of the earth where the dim rooms of our ances-
tors flicker. Their birds are there, and their crickets. The warm sand beneath
their feet. A picnic. A whale washed up on the beach breathing in all the air
around it, becoming solidity and dreamless sleep.

But they had dumb jokes, and personal identity. Half-baked ideas. I've seen
their magazines. They, too, sought pharmaceutical peace. Longed for sexual
release. It was not black and white, that world, despite the photographs. The
amputation saws. There were individual moments. A panoply! The discov-
ery of good luck. The invention of anxiety.

But even I who bring you the news cannot begin to believe it. The lost details
of their lives are also lost to me:

A white sack filled with black feathers.
A hole at the bottom of that sack.
Those black feathers drifting into an abyss of similar feathers.
Never, never to come back.

Thanksgiving

I want it back
Dying from the hunger of it
Stones in the Horn of Plenty
Cold in a gutter

But that's all just a little taste of death
The cornucopia pouring tender memories all over the family table
My perfumed mother in a new dress
My father confused with an electric knife
The seasonal feast, tasting like Time

Oh, my lucky platter, full once of nothing
Oh, my future tears in a dry cup once
All the little sufferings still to come
And the Great Loves
And the Great Loves

And we folded our hands in our laps, thanking Him

And we did it again
And we did it again

Mercy

The one unheated room in hell. The one
unhappy couple in heaven, screaming
obscenities at one another
on a street corner on the loveliest
day of summer:

Once, that was us. Happy anniversary. But

we got older, and the love took over. The
sunken luxury liner of so much.

So long *I'll never forgive you.*
So long *I want to kill you.*

What a joke:
An overcoat thrown out of the window
of a moving car. Wounds
to meat. Like

the Gorgon: A terrific

noise invented her.
Followed by silence.
A blaze of radiation
in a bedroom. Our mouths
left open. The way

they knocked the coliseum down
on the other side of town
and built a toy museum.

Little Christian.
Little lion.
Little cage.

Little door left open.

Right this way.

My son practicing the violin

Some farmers with their creaking machinery moving slowly across a field. Some geese. The sun rising somewhere on some unripe peaches. I wander the labyrinth of that orchard. The foxes creep out of their dens to peek at me. Even my high heels are green.

Such love, and such music, it's a wonder Jesus doesn't make me spend every waking hour on my knees.

We've traveled here from a distant planet to teach you how to be a human being.

Even the paper cup in my hand has learned to breathe. And each note is a beautiful, ancient kingdom precariously balanced at the edge of a cliff above the sea.

Stolen shoes

for the woman who stole my shoes
from the locker room at the gym

There is blood within the shoe
The shoe's too small for you

Such is the message in the cleft of the devil's foot
In the shrine piled high with sandals and pumps
In the shameless laughter of the younger women at Starbucks, leaning
      back, swinging their legs, full of foam, their cups

So much screaming in a small place
In a cage for a house cat, a cheetah

There is too much room in the shoe
The shoe's too big for you

The fish flopping in a bucket
Waddling through the orange grove, a wounded duck

So much screaming in that freedom
Butterfly on a windshield, clinging to a breeze

But, listen. I, too, stole something once only to stuff it in the trash

Together, me and you, thieves in one another's shoes at last

Or, better yet—
Have we *become* one another now, running barefoot in the grass

The mystical, final physics of that

Passion-in-July

I am the flower called Passion-in-July. Thirstless, yellow, growing in profusion under the awning of the condemned bordello in the morning.

No. *No.*

I bloom in the garden of the aging phys ed teacher in the middle of the night. She dreams of herself in the humid gymnasium, the walls lined with fur, the children running around her in mad circles. She wakes up not perspiring, but burning, singing, *Farewell, you cool violets in your shady hollows. You delicacies longing for water. I am the flower called Passion-in-July. Not sad. Not sky. If I could laugh, it would be*

in the face of the cemetery, virginity—those two mossy knolls.

It would be at the expense of the canvas shoe and its white laces, rubber soles.

Cigarettes

Back then, we smoked them. In
every family photo, someone's smoking.

Such ashes, such sarcasm, the jokes
that once made loved ones
who are dead now laugh and laugh.

Cigarette in hand.
Standing glamorously at the mantel.
The fire glowing
ahead and behind
and all the little glasses
and the snow outside

filling up the birdbaths, the open graves, the eyes.

And the orchestras in gymnasiums!
That mismanagement
of sound. The wonderful
smoke afterward
in parking lots, in lungs. How

homeliness was always followed
by extravagance back then.
Like hearing lovemaking
in another room
or passing suffering
on the side of the road
without even slowing down:

So it is to remember
such times
and to see them again
so vividly in the mind.
Like a mysterious child
traveling toward us
on a moonless night
holding a jar
containing a light.

Cytoplasm, June

The earth, spewing forth creatures.

Creatures, running wildly down mountainsides, stampeding over prairies, streaming from their holes and homes, frothing through rivers into lakes—feathers, fur, skin, hair, hooves, scales, claws. And all the subtle, separate emotions endured by them—expressed by lovers, induced by drugs. Birth, pain, terror. Humiliation. The terrible dull despair of a long drive through a large state beside a spouse who has grown over the decades to hate you.

Every morning we wake tethered to this planet by a rope around the ankle. Tied fast to a pole—but also loose, without rules, in an expanding universe. Always the dream of being a child afloat in the brilliant blue of the motel pool falling away, and an old man with cancer waking up on a bed of nails. *Please, don't remember me this way,* the world would like to say. And yet...

This is the entirety of the lesson. The lesson you learn from loving so greatly that which hath forsaken you:

It is a very, very small lesson. But not as small as you—

You, who are both a speck of dust drifting in silence out of the sky onto its brief gauzy wing, and the passing fancy of that passing damselfly.

Riddle

We are a little something, God's riddle seems to suggest.

Little memories.
Little wisdoms.
Little matches,
bright or snuffed.

Where did my grandmother go when she pulled her curtains closed?

I watched her window fade
from the backseat of my father's car, thinking
She is ancientness. She has lived forever. It has driven her insane.

But the New Old.
When did they grow
So Old?

Some of them are sleeping in the hallway.
Some are in their rooms
listening to rock 'n' roll.

This moment of wisdom, I cast you off.

This grand foolishness, I embrace you.

And my father—the kindest, cleanest
man I'll ever know—
is spitting on the floor, demanding to know where I came from.

THREE

The knot

The knot in the mind. That pounding thought. The cricket all night. That bright singing knot. That meditation on knots, which is a goat. The child who will be the knot of its love. This love like a knot concealed in a cloud. This death-obsessed knot with a backache, a knot-ache, holding its eye to a microscope. This loosening knot, and its greatest hope. This knot that is energy transferred into form. The knot of an eye. Not asleep. Not awake. But waiting, this knot. Like machinery parked beneath a tent made of gauze. This cramped signature on a piece of paper. A thickening knot. An egg like a knot. Not a fist in a lake, this knot of a stranger. Not the bureaucrat's stamp on the folder of our fate. But a knot nonetheless, and not of our making.

Animal, vegetable, mineral, mist

It rose all day over the snow
in the warm unseasonable *so.*
Evocative of *yes.* Suggestive
of *no.*

While the ants underground continued
their mindless knowing, and the children
in the sweatshop
went about their childish sewing.

The optimistic mist insists *There is a God.*
The pessimistic mist shrugs. *Perhaps
there is, but you'll never know.* And I

am reminded of the beautiful housekeeper at the seaside
resort so many years ago—

how busy she was flushing stars and doves
down the radiant toilet with her radiant wand
in waves and roars
in her gray clothes.

Too, the bit of fluff I watched
rise one Sunday morning from the hole
in a teenage boy's down coat, to float
through the whole cathedral, until
it reached the baptismal font

where it hovered for a long time before it came to rest
at the center of the sacred water, like a test.

And then
through my weird tears
a clear vision
at the center of the others:

My father
and the way for decades he drank his beer
beneath one bare bulb in a basement, like

a man desperately struggling to drown

a pale deer slowly in a shallow pond.

Riddle

The bodies of the girls in their beds, on their bikes, riding their horses through the clover, watching *Snow White,* sprawled on the rug chewing gum, reading Laura Ingalls Wilder—and, all the time, the chemical messages, the disseminated enzymes, the man in a tuxedo holding the door open wide, making that sweeping gesture with his arm.

Oh, biochemical seducers, hormonal wash, the external thyroid of a tadpole turning it irreversibly, involuntarily, into a frog.

They told us it was a dance, a party, a pageant, so we ran laughing together straight into the disaster. A pack of hounds dozed in the grass. Down the stairs, we ran, still wearing those glittering tiaras in our hair. Scaled Hadrian's Wall in our high heels. The hounds snapped their teeth in a dream. The geese overhead flew in formation, obeying the vague whisperings in their bird brains explaining to them the ridiculously complex rules of their own migrations.

While our mothers stood helplessly by and screamed,
and the farmers plowed their ancient fields,
and our fathers watched us from the front
porch

tapping their chins and wondering—
who were we?

Confession

Like an animal cut in half
Like its stomach full of stones

Like light pouring off of an accident—more light, and more

Like a shadow in a threshold
Like a document at the end of a corridor

Like human beings in pastures grazing
Like mourners, like horses
Like official violence

Torture

Like the hospital room of the child after the parents have left
Like facing your prom dress in your nakedness

Like facing Oblivion in your prom dress

Like black coffee spilled on the lilies
Like milk splashed onto the ashes

Here I come: The man dragging something

The thing he drags: Here I am

You

If you kept walking you would, eventually, step out of this blizzard. You would walk to the place where even a blizzard reaches its limits. The ragged edge of its sum total. The place it stops and says, *No more.*

And the sky, suddenly, would be, above you, unabashedly blue.

But here, the flakes still fall in their slow motion, wearing their geometries like trances. Perhaps no two are exactly alike, but they are also too alike to be given names, too much the same to be granted lives. They fall in crowds in the world as well as in the mind.

But you were beautiful, too, and free of illusions, so why—?

Well, I keep forgetting. You never listened to my suggestions. Never asked for my advice. When I built my luminous prison around you, you simply lay down at the center of it and died.

Abigor

He is the demon who knows all the secrets of war:
How a leader wins
the love of his soldiers.

He is also the puppet discarded on the floor.

And the dying dog
panting with the sound
of an empty basket
in the back yard.

He's the veranda on which the champagne kept flowing.
And the cool shade in which the witnesses
were tortured
until each one managed to tell a more

fantastic tale than the one before.

And the chiming of little birds
in the grass
just after—

And the guests gathered around the—

pretending to laugh.

And also the desperate
shrieks of the mink
caught in a trap
down by the creek

still with the swan's blood fresh on its teeth—

that unbearable song about the memory of that pleasure.

Forgiveness

Mercy, like the carcasses of animals in a foyer, being burned.

Fragrant, dreaming, unreal, and having to do, terribly, with love.

The sun shining dumbly all over this world and its troubles. The self on tip-
toes sneaking away from the self. In the passing lane today, a woman with
her mouth open behind the wheel of her car. Singing, or swearing, wearing
a coat, driving through her life, and mine.

Hello, little lifeboat made of straw. *Hello,* floating multitude of my sins in a
basket called Forgiveness on an ocean the name of which my son once mis-
pronounced the *Specific.*

Hello, ugly memory of myself crouched down with my fists on my thighs
yelling at that child:

Something about a stuffed animal and we're already late, and the palsied
trees of winter behind me reflected for thousands of miles in his eyes.

Pain pill

Today as the beauties slice across the frozen
lake in their bright skates, all
daggerish light in the distance, just
between swallowing
and sleeping, I'll—

One eye open in a grave.

One star over Bethlehem howling
over all the other stars.

Or the gray
spider sewing some old notion of herself between
the shade and the pane. The way

the memory of pain becomes
just that pale foam
left on the shore by the receding wave

or any of the other leftovers
of those Great Things
that meant you were alive
for a little while, and which
to love
would be too much, and to hate
would never be enough.

Now the skaters
are falling into dusk

one by one, as into wounds. Or
they skate on, but I can't see them. How, drunk, once
I stood in front
of my own door
unable to open it, until

finally I thought
(such deep thoughts)

Who's to say whether or not
I'm holding the wrong
key, or jamming
the right key
into someone else's lock?

That water that swallows us:

There is a heart
pumping at the center of it. So much
submerged thunder.
Or a match burning
between the pages of a book. Or a dove

with a pellet in its side, still
flying, still
wearing
its feathered self around it, but
undoing all memory

of flight
as it flies.

Almost there

The snail crossing the freeway in a rainstorm. A map might have helped. A more beautiful face. More life experience. Expensive perfume. A horse.

Given fewer options, and a grid. If not for uncertainty, the ancient Greeks, the ridiculous cheerfulness of sunflowers, the drifting immemorial ashes of the blueprints, the soup grown cold, the aunts gathered around the fiery cake, chanting, *Make a wish! Make a wish!*

The statistical index. The genetic predisposition. *If. If. If.*

Sing it all day long. Without it there is nothing but this code of lies, and the traffic of too much music in the mind. *If* is the diamond at the center of every life. The shining woman opening the window out of which her toddler will fall on a bright-white day in July:

Dad on a ladder outside.
Sister blabbing on the phone.
Not a cloud in the sky.
Not one thing wrong.
Almost there.
It is their song.

The Pleasure Center

It was tucked for us into the hypothalamus. *Thank you,* our lopped-off heads
rolling all around the earth. *Thank you,* radio, movies, booze.

And thank you, too, racquetball court, video game, throbbing bass in the car
at the stoplight as it pulls up next to ours.

Little fragment of a magnet.
Shrapnel in the attic.
Child on a bike.
Old woman on her knees beneath a suffering Jesus.
ADULT SUPERSTORE NEXT EXIT!

All of it crammed into a thing the size of a tadpole's eye.
That terrifying tininess. Thrilling, flickering, wet. Space and Time writhing
around in a bit of slippery shining. *God decided to stick that in our minds.*

And even the miniature golf course on fire.
The fatal dune buggy ride.
The smell of some teenage girl's menthol cigarette.
The whole amusement park, and the cotton candy—that
pink and painful sweetness beside you on the seat of some rollercoaster's
       silhouette
in the pinwheeling sun as it sets.

We were perfect test subjects for this.
As God is my witness:
I woke one morning when I was seven to find

the most unhappy man I've ever known
laughing in his pajamas. "What

are you laughing about?" I asked him,

and he said, "I don't know."

Lunch

has vanished. Just
a few crumbs on a plate, and the subway rumbling under us. It was

the Last Lunch. A bunch of us. We
would never be together in this life again.

A vein. A noose. A summer day. A rat crouching low
on the clattering tracks.

A storm. A scarf. A secret game. A man in the massive shadows
of the columns

of the Museum of Griefs-to-Come. A man
who would forever remain

our Observer, our Stranger
smirking in the corner of the photo behind our smug, shining faces.

Trees in fog

These trees in fog, not stirring, not calling:

How insistent they are
that they've been here all along
holding their tangible emptiness in their arms.

I admit it, I was wrong.

Here I stand, admitting it.

Like the mistress of the rich man
no longer in love
swallowing the pearls he gave her
one by one:

I was wrong.

But how I walked it—tenacity, my little dog—so
far and for so long. Walked

my wrongness all over the world.

Dressed it up.
Showed it off.

But that's all over now.

Now, I am a woman who realizes she was wrong.
And how wrong.

Now, I am a woman who would—

No.

Just throw me a veil.

Like them, I will bear it on the landscape.
I will wear it over the face.

Summer

She drank too much
She was after
Some meadow
Some orchard

Some childhood night with the window open, and it was summer, and her own mother was humming in another room, and through the screen the fuzzy blue, and suddenly she was out there swimming, too, in softness, a permanent candle, invisible, beautiful.

She drank too much
For many years
Some stairs
Some cosmetics
Once

I stood in the threshold and watched her disintegrate before a mirror.

My lovely mother before a tray full of bracelets
(*Repeat:* My lovely mother before a tray full of bracelets)

She invited me in to fish the ice cubes from her drink. They were warm. On my tongue. Such calm. Like a small bomb detonated in an isolated barn. Like a beloved pet in the middle of a busy street, simply standing there, looking around.

The organizers

That was the winter the organizers
got so businesslike about your death,
all the little Swiss watches glittering
so efficiently in the snow

The dice and the lots and the shuffled decks—
Goodbye to all that
It had been decided, been planned, precisely
even to the day, and to what you would be wearing, and to the last
word you would say, to the music on the radio at the nurse's station

For what purposes, then, the denial (that
bag of damp paperbacks and expired medications
shining and smudged in their amber vials)

Except that it was mine
And still I walk the sidewalk mumbling

something about how it will all be fine

Fine is its own crazy village on the Rhine
Fine is the name of the cuckoo-clock maker
Fine is the word the cuckoo cries

     every hour after hour on the hour—
     scrambling out of its dark little hole

     like something being chased with a knife by Time

Four men

1

Too late.
The gods of old Greece
have been reduced to this
disease, stuffed
into a dusty cupboard
in a kitchen full of shit.

I used to scramble after that on my hands and knees.
I used to beg for it over and over.

If not for the longing
and the ire, and the long day tethered to your ankle by a chain—

would you have come home earlier, and sober?

2

Men differ:
locally, and wither. We

sat up all night
arguing.

Men are the same:
the universe, and live forever. We

slept in each other's arms all day.

3

For a while you wore
your bloody regalia
everywhere you went. All

muscle and movement wrapped
in a damp scarlet blanket. Crowded

offices, and wide-open spaces.
I couldn't take it.

I told you a tasteless joke, and you hated it.

I wanted to see
what would happen if I took down your fortress
nail by nail. Then

brick by brick. *My*

warm breath on your neck.

I told the joke again.

4

Furious rain on a furious lake.
The year of our waste.
Ashes in an ashtray in a burning bar,
and a man holding a woman made of bad moods in his arms.

I made a mockery of you.
You made a laughingstock of me.
A subtle love. The heart. Its
iambic, jellied waves.

Who knew those bees were making
honey of our grief? Who knew
that the workmen,
hired to be fair, would knock down the airy
wall one morning
between us
and neither of us would be there?

Briefly

Here and there some scrap of beauty gets snatched from this or that: One
child's voice rising above the children's choir. A few wild notes of laughter
passing through the open window of a passing car. That pink handkerchief
waved at the parade. The tiny Nile-blue tile broken at the edge of the mosaic
—all shining accident and awe. And this

last second or two of dreaming
in which your face
returns to me completely. Not
even needing to be, being

so alive again to me.

They say

one-twelfth of our lives is wasted
standing in a line.

The sacred path of that.

Ahead of me, a man in black, his broad back.
Behind me, a woman like me
unwinding her white veils.

And beyond us all, the ticket-taker, or the old
lady with our change, or

the officials with our food, our stamps, our unsigned papers, our
gas masks, our inoculations.

It hasn't happened yet.
It hasn't begun or ended.
It hasn't granted us its bliss
or exploded in our faces.
The baby watches the ceiling from its cradle.
The cat stares at the crack in the foundation.
The grandfather flies the sick child's kite higher
and higher. I set

my husband's silverware on the table.

I place a napkin beside my son's plate.

Soon enough,
but not tonight.
Ahead of us, that man's black back.
Behind us, her white veils.

Ahead of us, the nakedness, the gate.

Behind us, the serene errand-boy, the cigarette, the wink-
and-nod, the waiting.

Beyond that, too late.

Receipt

The cat rips the couch to pieces with the claws he's forgotten he no longer
has. Air, so much heavier than memory, which returns again and again to its
nurseries, and factories, and sweetly winding garden paths. Outside, in the
sky, a plane filled with the traveling dead soars by.

The couch has been torn to pieces, scattered in ruined fragments all over the
floor. What the cat once curled upon. What the cat will lie upon once more.

How lucky to be spared from one's own impulses.
And how terrible.

The way, myself, this afternoon, cleaning out a drawer, I came upon the
receipt for that wrecked thing we used to love, and also found unbearable.

Life support

A planet made of only ocean
    and the only boat on that ocean loaded only with mirrors and stones

Foil wrapped around a tragedy
The tragedy, wrapped in foil
A tragic voice inside a brick, and also the brick
    Let me out
    Let me in

Why *not* the Victorians and their sentimental grief-wreaths woven from a
loved one's hair?

Gall bladder, as goblin
Liver as dirty pet
Lungs panting like featherless squabs in a net
The spleen, that bloody jokester
The stomach, Brueghel's monkey on a chain
The heart hacked out of the center of an overgrown hedge with an ax
To live beyond the brain:

A sack of feathers, claws, and fingernails

Turn the corner, and there she is:
The pretty little girl who asked you for a kiss you wouldn't give
That undiscovered country someone scissored from the map:

Now, that's where you live

Incredible, how it all goes on without you
Behold the torn wrapping paper and the ribbons on the floor
Behold the gifts:

The bees liberated from their hives
        buzzing in ashes on the ground
A painting of a passionate embrace
        on a broken vase
My memory of your casual smile

This memory, like
        a child's bit of sweet embroidery smuggled
        out of an asylum

My father's mansion

We were adolescents, after school. We prowled the grounds of an abandoned mansion. It was a museum devoted entirely to our empty dreams. Except that we were simply, still, golden, steaming shapes against the snow, and then the green. And this abandoned mansion was the mind, exposed, like the guts and excrement of an animal in the road. The pear tree had gone crazy. The one carp in the pond had starved. A boy I loved climbed onto the roof of the mansion and pounded on his chest. He shouted down, "I'm King Kong!" and then, thinking even harder about the situation we were in, shouted even louder, "No. I'm God!"

Heart/mind

A bear batting at a beehive, how

clumsy the mind
always was with the heart. Wanting
what it wanted.

The blizzard's
accountant, how
timidly the heart approached the business
of the mind. Counting
what it counted.

Light inside a cage, the way the heart—

Bird trapped in an airport, the way the mind—

How it flashed on the floor of the phone booth, my
last dime. And

this letter
I didn't send
how surprising

to find it now.

All this love I must have felt.

Riddle

Most days I cling to a single word. It is a mild-mannered creature made of thought. *Future,* or *Past.* Never the other, obvious word. Whenever I reach out to touch that one, it scurries away.

Even my identity has been kept hidden from me. It is a child's ghost buried in mud. It is an old woman waving at me from a passing train. First, a multiplication. Then, a densification. Then, a pale thing draped carelessly over a bone.

Four weeks after my conception, I was given a tail. But then God had some mystical vision of all I might be—and took the tail back.

It required no violence, no surgery, no struggle, this quiet thievery, this snatching away of the deep, ancient secret. It would be true of everything:

My eyes closed, hands open, *Take it, take it.* Then, every day wasted chasing it.

Love poem

The water glass. The rain. The scale
waiting for the weight. The car.
The key. The rag. The dust. Once

I was a much younger woman
in a hallway, and I saw you:

I said to myself
Here he comes.
My future's husband.

And even before that. I was the pink
throbbing of the swim bladder
inside a fish in the River Styx. I was
the needle's eye. I was the air
around the wing of a fly, and you

had no idea you were even alive.

Tools and songs

Behind the apple trees, beyond the house, in the neighbor's field, beneath a starless sky, at the edge of the woods, on a night in February, after the ice storm, but still a few hours before the terrible news, I hear the coyotes howling those excited prepositions that are

art and government and bad decisions.

Fishhooks, arrowheads, knitting needles, and the small dull words that connect these scrawny godless dogs and their dogless gods to me.

In my kitchen. In my nightgown. In my role as mother and wife. My hand on the teapot, an orangutan's. My bare feet on the floor, a chimpanzee's. I have a few simple tasks I can do without tools that were not given selflessly to me—as the coyotes out there laugh and hiccup and confess it all:

The rabbit and the barn-cat and the quivering mole. The wild geese and the old woman's poodle and the child's pet sheep. A few decades' worth of shameless memories in the mind of someone's thankless daughter. *God, please—*

Give me a set of simple tools out of which to fashion a song for these.

Home

It would take forever to get there
but I would know it anywhere:

My white horse grazing in my blossomy field.
Its soft nostrils. The petals
falling from the trees into the stream.

The festival would be about to begin
in the dusky village in the distance. The doe
frozen at the edge of the grove:

She leaps. She vanishes. My face—
She has taken it. And my name—

(Although the plaintive lark in the tall
grass continues to say and to say it.)

Yes. This is the place.
Where my shining treasure has been waiting.
Where my shadow washes itself in my fountain.

A few graves among the roses. Some moss
on those. An ancient

bell in a steeple down the road
making no sound at all
as the monk pulls and pulls on the rope.

Lannan Literary Selections

For two decades Lannan Foundation has supported the
publication and distribution of exceptional literary works.
Copper Canyon Press gratefully acknowledges their support.

LANNAN LITERARY SELECTIONS 2011

Michael Dickman, *Flies*

Laura Kasischke, *Space, in Chains*

Deborah Landau, *The Last Usable Hour*

Valzyhna Mort, *Collected Body*

Dean Young, *Fall Higher*

RECENT LANNAN LITERARY SELECTIONS
FROM COPPER CANYON PRESS

Stephen Dobyns, *Winter's Journey*

David Huerta, *Before Saying Any of the Great Words: Selected Poems*,
translated by Mark Schafer

Sarah Lindsay, *Twigs and Knucklebones*

Heather McHugh, *Upgraded to Serious*

W.S. Merwin, *Migration: New & Selected Poems*

Taha Muhammad Ali, *So What: New & Selected Poems, 1971–2005*,
translated by Peter Cole, Yahya Hijazi, and Gabriel Levin

Travis Nichols, *See Me Improving*

Lucia Perillo, *Inseminating the Elephant*

James Richardson, *By the Numbers*

Ruth Stone, *In the Next Galaxy*

John Taggart, *Is Music: Selected Poems*

Jean Valentine, *Break the Glass*

C.D. Wright, *One Big Self: An Investigation*

For a complete list of Lannan Literary Selections from
Copper Canyon Press, please visit Partners on our Web site:
www.coppercanyonpress.org

About the Author

Laura Kasischke (pronounced Ka-ZISS-kee) was raised in Grand Rapids, Michigan. She attended the University of Michigan, where she received her B.A. and her M.F.A. in creative writing. She is now an associate professor there, in the Residential College and the M.F.A. program, and lives in Chelsea, Michigan, with her husband and son. A writer of fiction as well as poetry, she has published eight novels, two of which have been made into feature films—*The Life before Her Eyes* and *Suspicious River*—and eight books of poetry. She has received fellowships from the Guggenheim Foundation and the National Endowment for the Arts, as well as several Pushcart Prizes.

 Since 1972, Copper Canyon Press has fostered the work of emerging, established, and world-renowned poets for an expanding audience. The Press thrives with the generous patronage of readers, writers, booksellers, librarians, teachers, students, and funders — everyone who shares the belief that poetry is vital to language and living.

Copper Canyon Press gratefully acknowledges board member

JIM WICKWIRE

in honor of his many years of service to poetry and independent publishing.

NATIONAL
ENDOWMENT
FOR THE ARTS

WASHINGTON STATE
ARTS COMMISSION

Major support has been provided by:

Amazon.com

Anonymous

Beroz Ferrell & The Point, LLC

Golden Lasso, LLC

Lannan Foundation

Rhoady and Jeanne Marie Lee

National Endowment for the Arts

Cynthia Lovelace Sears and Frank Buxton

William and Ruth True

Washington State Arts Commission

Charles and Barbara Wright

*To learn more about underwriting
Copper Canyon Press titles, please call
360-385-4925 x103*

The Chinese character for poetry is made up of two parts: "word" and "temple." It also serves as press-mark for Copper Canyon Press.

The text is set in Aldus, designed by Hermann Zapf. The heads are set in Legato, designed by Evert Bloemsma. Book design and composition by Valerie Brewster, Scribe Typography. Printed on archival-quality paper at McNaughton & Gunn, Inc.